Launch Your Book into the Stratosphere & be a Best Seller!

Richter Publishing

Write & Publish a Book Series

(Volume IV)

By Tara Richter

Published by Richter Publishing LLC www.richterpublishing.com

Edited by Casey Cavanagh, Ricardo Angulo, Ke'Shawnda Chambers

Copyright © 2015 Richter Publishing LLC

ISBN:0692425330
ISBN-13:9780692425336

DISCLAIMER

This book is designed to provide information on writing and marketing only. This information is provided and sold with the knowledge that the publisher and author do not offer any legal or medical advice. In the case of a need for any such expertise, consult with the appropriate professional. This book does not contain all information available on the subject. This book has not been created to be specific to any individual's or organization's situation or needs. Every effort has been made to make this book as accurate as possible. However, there may be typographical and/ or content errors. Therefore, this book should serve only as a general guide and not as the ultimate source of subject information. This book contains information that might be dated and is intended only to educate and entertain. The author and publisher shall have no liability or responsibility to any person or entity regarding any loss or damage incurred, or alleged to have incurred, directly or indirectly, by the information contained in this book. You hereby agree to be bound by this disclaimer or you may return this book within the guarantee time period for a full refund. In the interest of full disclosure, this book contains affiliate links that might pay the author or publisher a commission upon any purchase from the company. While the author and publisher take no responsibility for the business practices of these companies and or the performance of any product or service, the author or publisher has used the product or service and makes a recommendation in good faith based on that experience. Any and all references to Amazon, TBBJ or other companies including screenshots, is owned solely by them. This is just a reference guide to teach others how to utilize their systems.

All characters appearing in this work are fictitious. Any resemblance to real persons, living or dead, is purely coincidental.

FOREWORD

"I was so excited to be one of Tara's clients to be coached through the writing and publishing process! I have never written a book, so I knew when I wanted to embark on this journey, she was the one I needed to contact. Since she already had three books under her belt, I called her to find out how she did it. I was amazed after our phone conversation that she had discovered a quick and easy way to get a book published in only a few months. I didn't even think that was possible! I knew Kevin and I had to work with her on our project. I really wanted our book to come from the heart and soul so it would resonate with the reader. It was a challenging journey, but Tara's tips and coaching has really made the process a breeze. She's helped us every step of the way and looked out for me, Tara keeps me on track with my goal. If I can write and publish a book with no experience, you can too!"

- *Anthony Amos Multi-Founding Franchisor & Partnership Expert*

http://theanthonyamos.com/

"When Anthony and I decided to publish a joint book, he said he wanted it to be available for sale within a few months. I thought he was crazy, we wouldn't have enough time in our hectic schedules to get this done. However, when we brought Tara aboard, her coaching techniques made it easy. She has streamlined the writing and publishing process, utilizing every spare minute for maximum results. Even with my super busy schedule I can get a book done. She utilizes every spare second you have. If you want to be a published author, Tara is the one to get the job done!"

- *Kevin Harrington, Shark from ABC's "Shark Tank"*

http://kevinharrington.tv/

CONTENTS

INTRODUCTION

You finally got your book in your hands! Congratulations! You are now officially a published author and an expert in your field! You might ask, *Now what? What's next?* The next phase of our journey into publishing is self-promotion—launching your book into the stratosphere! I will walk you through the steps of how to plan, market and capitalize the success of your first book launch party and become an Amazon Best Seller.

You want your book to reach a wide audience and to ultimately generate a following. Here you will learn how to do everything from throwing a book launch party, to gaining media attention, and even getting celebrity appearances! In the following chapters, I concoct a great recipe for a soaring launch with 10 powerful ingredients.

Planning and executing a great book release has the potential to pave the way for future successes. For my first book launch party, I was literally on my own and had to start from scratch. I had to be smart and gather my resources without having a big budget. By my second launch party, I landed a celebrity guest appearance, and by my third party, I gained full sponsorship of my events. Planning prosperous events is a lot of work, but there *is* a method to the madness.

I will walk you through the same steps I took to plan and market each of my events, and show you how to fully utilize the resources around you to ensure the success of your first book release. By the end of this manual, you will know exactly what it takes to launch your book into the stratosphere and become a Best Seller, newly published author. First I'm going to share with you my 10 ingredients for a fruitful book launch party, then dive into Best Seller status.

So what are you waiting for? Let's get started!

Sincerely,

Tara Richter

INGREDIENT 1: A GREAT LOCATION

Location, location, location! The venue is one of the main parts of the event. That's where people are going to show up. Make sure the venue is centrally located so it's easy to find. A popular place is usually easier, because people will already be familiar with where it is. Make sure the space can accommodate the number of guests you are expecting. Interact with the manager and staff at the venue so you know they are cooperative. The last thing you want to do is clash with the owner or manager—it will make your event a nightmare!

Find out the basics and ask a lot of questions. Will they charge you to rent this space? Do you have to buy food and drinks from them? Can you provide your own food? Do they have parking? Do you have to use valet service or is there street parking? Knowing all the "extra" pieces of info makes it easier to accommodate your guests. You need to know how much street parking is. Or parking garages are close by. Do they have parking to accommodate 200 cars? Do they have relationships with nearby places for discounts?

Securing a location is easy. Find a place that is new, a location that needs the exposure. Let's say a bakery opened up in town. Talk to them. They want more exposure for their business, and you can provide that for them. Recently-opened locations welcome the sudden burst of customers. With your help, you can make that a reality!

Hold the event on an off-night, such as a Monday, Tuesday or Wednesday. Most bars or restaurants are slow on those nights, so they will welcome the traffic. If your venue has a cash bar, keep track of your totals. At the Jazz café for my first book launch party, I asked the manager what the sales were for the party. We only had 25 people show up. The bar tab was over $3,000. That revenue is an incentive for your future book launch parties. Business owners will let you use their space for free, because you have evidence that you will bring them the profit they need.

If you want to put your event on the map, have it at a prestigious location. For example, a high-end car dealership. That space would be a ton of fun. Who wouldn't want the chance to hang out around these beautiful luxury cars? Photographers would take pictures of people's cars. Of course, you will have luxurious memories to take with you.

Also consider the weather and time of year. Is it nice enough to have it outdoors or will it be indoors? For one of my Author Awards Ceremonies, I choose a beautiful location on the waterfront in Clearwater. The view was gorgeous, the space was big, the price was right and we could bring in our own food and drinks. One of the things I

2

didn't consider was daylight savings time. It was the first weekend in November. The event went from 6pm-9pm. I was planning on having a great view of the gorgeous sunset over the water. The week prior I was on a radio show and they were discussing that we had to move our clocks. As I was sitting there on the air my head started to spin. "Oh my God! It's going to get dark at 6pm. My event is going to be pitch black! No one will see the sunset!"

That's exactly what happened. Well, all the authors, vendors and people working the event saw the sunset, but no one else. It was pitch black and you could only see shimmers of light dance across the ocean. At the last minute, I had to scramble and grab small lighted trees, strings of Christmas lights and any illuminated decorations from my house to put around the tables so people could see! It was crazy and hectic, but we pulled it off.

However, our guest count was down a lot from our previous event. And I think a telling factor was that, even though it was gorgeous, it was too far away. No one wanted to drive over two bridges to get to it during the week. Some who did try to make it had a hard time finding it. Even though there was a sign lit up with our info, many people passed right by it because it was so dark. This is another reason why having a popular location is better. No matter what the weather, people will know where it's located.

Above is me and one of the authors, Elizabeth Norlin, at the Author Awards Ceremony. We started taking pictures early to get some sunlight in. You can see the beautiful view in the back that only lasted until the event started.

Things to consider when choosing a venue:

- Is it centrally located, so most people can attend?
- Is the owner/manager/staff cooperative?
- Will they charge you?
- Can you provide your own food and drinks?
- Is the venue easily accessible?
- Will the parking situation be a problem?
- What time of year will it be?

INGREDIENT 2: A DATE TO REMEMBER

Pick a memorable date. Your party should stick in people's mind. By tying your event with a notable holiday, you will earn more exposure, and more people will remember your party.

Associate it with something we all know: July 4th, New Years, Valentine's Day, etc. If you can't pick a holiday, try to pick a date with repeating numbers, like 12/12/2012. Anything that guests can cling to.

For my first party, I tied the event with Halloween. It was held a week before the actual celebration of the dead. Since it was close by, everyone was in the mood to dress up in costumes. My *Dating Jungle* books are geared towards single people. What do single people like to do? Get dressed up, go out for drinks, meet people and have fun! So that's exactly what my party was. Everything I like to do when I'm single. Costume parties are always a blast. My first book launch was a "Singles

Mixer Costume Contest." We all dressed up like animals from the jungle or Jane and Tarzan. I dressed up as Jane, and one man came as Tarzan. Let me tell you, he *really* was wearing *only* a loin cloth. I'll spare you the photo of that one!

It was a hoot though! I got many people to come out who I had never met before. As a first time author, that's a great sign! It's always important to keep track of your marketing results as well. So as I sold books and mixed with the crowd, I made sure to ask the guests where they heard about the party.

My second book launch party, I actually held it on Valentine's Day. If you're single, Valentine's Day can be a bummer. So the event was a singles mixer at a bar. There were drinks and treats. I gave single people a reason to come out on this holiday. The occasion was a great way to connect with my book, *10 Rules to Survive the Internet Dating Jungle.*

The first event I held for free. The second event I charged a cover fee since it was a singles affair. There are a lot of singles happenings to meet other people and they always charge a fee. I figured mine should be no different, that people would still come out and I was right! The first event I lost money, but my second event I made $400. Not a huge amount, but every little bit counts!

The first Author Awards Ceremony we held before the holidays, in the very first week of November. The planning behind that date was because once the holidays come around, everyone is too busy planning for them. Plus with holiday parties and relatives in town, everyone's schedule gets packed. The other reason is guests will be thinking of buying Christmas presents. That's what they're in the mood for. I even suggested to the vendors and authors to have some books pre-wrapped so it's ready for holiday gift giving!

Associate your event with a holiday or event. Create an attention grabber. Anything to secure your event as a remarkable occasion. Another key thing to remember when booking your event is research to see if there are any other BIG events going on that same time. You don't want to have to compete with any major events in your area. For example in Tampa we have our annual "Gasparilla Parade." It draws a huge crowd. So I wouldn't have my event the same weekend because, for one, traffic is going to be nuts and you don't want to get tied up in it. Second, most people are attending it. I wouldn't even do it the day afterwards because people are tired or hungover. Plus if your event would be in the same area, parking can be a pain. So make sure to look up and be familiar with big events so nothing conflicts. Ask your event planner at the venue as well. If they are a seasoned coordinator, they should know all this information. They should know of any and all conflicts. That's their job. If they don't, you might want to choose another venue. They are responsible for making your party happen as smoothly as possible.

However, you need to do your own due diligence as well. Check your local Chambers of Commerce or other big associations. If any of them do annual events, they usually stick to the same date range. I know all the major players in Tampa and I know their big event schedules. I plan my Author Awards Ceremony on a date when nothing else major is going on. It's just smart. Sometimes though you can't always avoid other peoples' plans. So make the best educated decision you can, then book it—far in advance. For a wedding, they tell you to book it a year out. For other big events, that seem almost like a wedding, I book it six months out. Most important things to book: 1) the date 2) the venue. Get those items done first! Then you can promote the hell out of it.

INGREDIENT 3: PRIZES

Giving away gifts is another great way to get more business involved in your event. It is always a hit.

Contact local businesses and see if they would like to give away a gift certificate or gift bag with products to promote their company. Rising business are always interested in getting more attention for their services. So don't be shy about asking! You never know what you will get in return. People always want to get their name in the headlines, so if you can promote your sponsors in the media, that's always a bonus and selling point.

You *could* give away books as prizes. Don't give away a lot, though, because you want to make *money* on them. Maybe just do one packaged with some coaching sessions. Books are products that you have to pay for. Services, like a coaching session, is your time. And yes, time is money. However, most likely when you give away an hour phone instruction lesson, people never even redeem them. It's funny how the brain works. Even if you put a value of $100 on that session, for some reason when a person "wins" it and they pay no money, they have no investment in it. So they discard it. As if it has no value, but it does. They could learn a wealth of information for FREE. But most people will not take you up on it. It's the human psyche that tells us FREE = no value. Hence why products are priced at certain levels. The whole $12.99 or $19.99—that one cent makes a difference. Thus, FREE = no good.

Obviously your coaching session (or whatever service you provide) has value, but just printing service and value on a piece of paper—a certificate—makes it LOOK like you're giving a lot away. SMART people would jump at the chance. I know I do. Anytime I can get into something FREE I jump at it. I've gotten free tickets to seminars that cost thousands of dollars. Free sessions, discounted stuff and then I absorb as much as I can from the experience and move on.

So the point I'm making here is that you can give away an abundance of items that really only cost the paper the gift card is printed on. Your out-of-pocket costs are low. And expenses are something you have to watch when having an event. I know all too well how to throw a party on a shoe string budget. It's okay. We've all been there—that time when you are struggling to make ends meet. You want to watch your resources. It's a smart thing to do. Keep costs low so you can make a profit. At the end of the day that's what it's about. And there's no reason to be ashamed about that. This isn't a non-profit, this is your life. You are sharing your gifts with the world. You deserve compensation for that. Your talents and gifts are there to keep a roof over your head. That doesn't happen by always giving them away for free; be selective.

Someone advised me to give my books away for free at my first launch. But it's a book promotion party. People are coming to *buy* your book. When you give them away for free, you earn nothing. Always charge something. In person, I charge twenty dollars for an autographed copy. You want people to know that your blood, sweat and tears deserves compensation.

An irritating fact once you are an author: People who meet you sometimes think you should give your book to them for free. Why? Where does that come from? People don't realize the time it took to create the work that is now neatly printed and bound within their hands. Just because they can hold 30,000 words that were torn from your soul in their grip, doesn't mean they shouldn't compensate you. They didn't see the endless nights and torturous hours after the many edits and revisions. They think it's just, *Poof! Here's a book*. Well sometimes that happens, more so not—unless you use my company. (Shameless plug.) So YES! Make people buy your book ALWAYS.

T-Shirts are great prizes as well. I had Dating Jungle T-Shirts made for my *Dating Jungle Series* events. People wear them in public, getting you more exposure. So make sure your T-Shirts are great advertisements for your book.

There are many different types of prizes. People will like anything: bottles of wine, photoshoots, cruises, you name it. I barter with my hair stylist for my events. He will style my hair for free. In exchange, he advertises his business on my flyers and for the party. He brings gift baskets filled with hair products to raffle. I promote him, he provides prizes. It's a win-win.

Here are a few examples of prizes:

- T-Shirts
- Books
- Gift Certificates
- Gift Baskets
- Free Coaching Sessions
- Bottles of Wine
- Photoshoots
- Cruises
- Membership Trials

INGREDIENT 4: CHARITY INVOLVEMENT

Positivity. Every event needs it. A charity is a great encouraging draw for your party. Not only do you raise money for a good cause, but you can garner media attention. Your event becomes well-rounded. People will want to attend your event, and you will also make a difference in your community.

For my third and fourth book launch party, we had the organization The Kind Mouse in attendance. (http://thekindmouse.org/)

The organization assists families in Tampa Bay who are struggling through transitions. The Kind Mouse helps feed these families by donating food and school lunches. We always have one charity able to come out and set up a table for free to get exposure for their cause and to help raise money by donations.

Once you get to the level where you can get 200 people to come out to your party, it's great to give back to your community. You can use the same charity or rotate through different ones.

If you sell tickets to your event, part of the proceeds can be donated to the charity. Or if you raffle off prizes, those sales can go to them as well. There's all types of ways to get the community involved and do progressive things to help multiple people.

If your book is about something you overcame, such as breast cancer, involving an organization with that aspect would be a great addition to your party.

INGREDIENT 5: CELEBRITIES

Celebrities are a great addition to your book launch party. It might sound difficult, but it's actually not that hard. Celebrities come in all shapes and sizes, and they will bring the notoriety you need for your party.

For my second book launch party, my first location fell through. We found a new location at The Slug, a bar in Westchase. The manager's cousin was none other than David Good, from the TV hit reality series *The Bachelor Pad* and *The Bachelorette*.

We asked the manager to contact him to see if he would come out for half an hour or so to hang out at the party. It was Valentine's Day, so it was a little bit much to ask him to take time away from his plans for the night. However, it turned out The Slug was Good's local hangout spot. So David brought his girlfriend and some friends out. They stayed for hours, having a lot of fun. I think he had more fun at my book launch party than I did!

The cool thing is, Good is also a published author. Which I didn't even know. He published a book titled *The Man Code* after his success on *The Bachelor Pad*. His stint on *The Bachelorette* show was not long. However, he was on the very first season of *The Bachelor Pad* where previous TV reality stars got to compete, this time for prizes instead of love. David ended up winning the grand prize with his teammate Natalie Getz of $250,000!

He brought some of his books out to the party. We had a nice chat about being authors and his time on the shows. He and his girlfriend were very nice and a pleasure to have at the party.

So it's not as difficult as it may seem to get somebody with a little bit of fame out to support your party. It's the whole six degrees of separation theory. I hired an event planner, he knew the manager at the bar, talked about the theme of my party, and his cousin was on TV. BAM that easy. So start asking around. You have no idea who you know, whose brother or sister or aunt may have gone to school with whomever. Really anything in this world is possible. We just have to ASK for it!

At my first collaborative book launch party as Richter Publishing LLC, we had Kevin Harrington from ABC's *Shark Tank* in attendance and Brian Ripka, son of Judith Ripka, the famous jewelry line on QVC.

I was working on a book title *How to Catch a Shark* with "Shark Bites" from Kevin Harrington, authored by Anthony Amos. Both of them came out to promote their upcoming book at the party. Anthony Amos has a business where he's partners with Kevin Harrington and Brian Ripka called, Bellebrations. They just so happened to be in town, so they all came out to the book launch. Once you know people at certain levels they are going to always be associating themselves with the same crowds. Hence, you are who you hang out with. So hang out in influential crowds! Having all of them there was a great, they gave the party more credibility, and it definitely helped draw more guests. People flock to famous people. By leveraging star power, our company had a grander stature.

We had almost 200 people pack the room that night. It was a fantastic event! Everyone was taking pictures and posting them all over social media. I had people calling me up for a week after the fact saying, "How did I NOT know about this event?!" That's the kind of pull you want! People talking about it for days afterwards.

INGREDIENT 6: MEDIA ATTENTION

Always get media attention on your party. The more media attention you receive, the more sales you will earn.

I had no clue what I was doing for my first party. I printed up flyers and posted them everywhere. Literally. Wherever I went, there was a trail of flyers behind me. Malls, stores, bookstores, bars. I attended four costume parties with a custom QR code on my butt for people to scan. When they scanned it, the party would come up, and when people asked about it, I gave them a flyer. Those flyers littered Tampa Bay.

I posted about the event on multiple websites. I even submitted the event on the *Bays News 9* Community Calendar for free (http://www.baynews9.com/content/news/baynews9/community/community-calendar.html). They chose to feature my event on *Bay News 9* neighborhood news.

Get your party details out there as much as possible. The more places it's listed, the more people hear about it. Use social media. There are many free places within your community that are looking for local events.

I listed my event on several websites:

- Creative Loafing
  http://posting.cltampa.com/tampa/Events/AddEvent
- Event Live
  https://www.eventliveus.com/
- 813 Area Events
  www.813area.com/events
- Eventbrite
  https://www.eventbrite.com

Search your local area for websites that list social events. Concentrate on how you advertise the event. Include the necessary information. Focus on fun. For example, "Jazz bar," "Party," "Prizes." All of these things get people excited to come out and enjoy your event.

For my second party, I hired a PR guy. I wanted TV interviews, so he got me one on *Channel 10 News*, which aired two hours before the party. A lot of people came out because they heard about the event through my interview. Imagine how I felt when the bartender pointed at the TV, said "That's you!" Imagine how I felt when the phone rang and peopled asked, "Where is this bar?" "How do I get there?"

I did not hire a PR guy for my third book launch party. One of my authors actually was a PR guy, James Chittenden with Triumph Business Communications. He published his book through my company, so he helped us score media attention for the collaborative book launch. We went to the offices of *The Tampa Tribune*, a major newspaper in town,

A cake made like a stack of books was the centerpiece of a refreshments table at a book launch party on April 8. LENORA LAKE

and physically spoke to some of the Community News Reporters. LENORA LAKE Tribune correspondent, came out to the party, took photos and did coverage on the event.

When you are trying to get media attention yourself, it's sometimes easier to get the reporters to come out by approaching them on a one-on-one interaction. By narrowing down the type of event you have and who would be interested in covering it, as reporters are usually covering certain types of stories. If you write up a press release, then email blast it out to various outlets without first finding out if they would even *consider* that type of event, you might just be wasting your time. However, if you research the person who would be interested in your affairs, then customize the approach towards them, your actions can be more productive.

James also was able to use this approach to get *The Tampa Bay Business Journal* to come out, interview me, as well as some of the other authors. Marjorie Manning, a Print Editor for the *Tampa Bay Business Journal*, did a fabulous job with the article. Now I have established a great relationship with her where I send her a direct email when we have events going on. This is the type of relationship you want to have with reporters. To make their job and life easier. Reporting on stories is their job. They are constantly looking for new happenings to put into the news. Something that's going to grab people's attention. Another reason why your party must be fun, entertaining and a little different: so they will *want* to cover you.

Tampa Bay Business Journal article & short video posted online after the event.

For example, one day I was driving to the post office and I heard on the radio that *Channel 8 News* here in Tampa was doing a segment on the evening news about online dating. Well since I'm most likely one of the only authors in the Tampa Bay area who has written and published a book on the subject matter, and had a radio show, I would be an excellent resource for information. So when I got home I went to their website, looked up the reporters name and gave her a call. Of course she didn't answer the phone herself, they have a secretary or some other gate keeper. Since I wanted to make sure I got through to the right person, I made sure I had my "short pitch" perfect so I wouldn't get shut down. It basically went a little bit like this:

"Hello, *Channel News 8*. This is Stephanie, how can I help you?"

"Hi, I'm Tara Richter, local published author of *10 Rules to Survive the Internet Dating Jungle.* I just heard on the radio one of your news reporters is doing a segment tonight on online dating. I was wondering if she needed some help with information from an expert in the industry?"

"Okay sure," said Stephanie. "Let me put you through."

The phone rang and I was sent directly to the reporter covering that story. We chatted on the phone for a good 20-30 minutes and she asked me a ton of questions for more information. She said she was so happy I called in and that I was a wealth of information. I was excited to share my knowledge with someone reputable. She took down my contact info for future stories, thanked me and hung up the phone. I excitedly watched the news that night and MY tips were shared on the news that night! However, my name, book or credits to that information was not. So there's a few lessons to be learned here. It's easier than you think to contact media sources and get your name into TV, newspapers and online. But also make sure you tell the reporter that if they *do use* your insight, they give you credit as the source.

Another interesting incident I had was a lady who won my *Dating Jungle Book Series* in a raffle. She was married so she thought she had no use for my books. She gave one of them away, then read the Internet Dating one for fun. It so happened for some strange reason that she was asked to be interviewed on a TV show about internet dating even though she had no experience. She accepted (not sure why), but used all the tips from my book without quoting me or giving me credit for her resource. I had no idea any of this even happened until I ran into her at a conference and she came up to me and told me the story. I had never met the woman in my life and the look of horror on my face as she told me what she did explained it all. Never use someone's story and experiences without giving them the credit. It's immoral, unethical and just downright rude. Also, in some cases, against the law. Give credit where credit is due and make sure you request that of anyone you are helping out in the media realm. It's just common courtesy.

Maureen Pelamati, a Robinson High School English teacher, talks with James Chittenden, author of "The Public Triumph," at a book launch party April 8. LENORA LAKE

The next few photos are also from the *Tampa Tribune* article that was published after the event. Even if the media attention is after the fact, it raises your online profile. You receive more credibility. When people research your name, they can see that you know what you're doing.

You definitely want to track and keep the articles, photos or videos that are posted after your event. You need to repurpose that information. So even if people missed the event, they can still see how great it was. They will probably be sad to miss it when "everyone" was there! Repurposing the articles is easy. Post links on your social media accounts, write a blog with them in it and even send out an event follow

Author Joseph Warren talks with guests at an April 8 book launch party, which included his book, What's in it for Me? LENORA LAKE

up email. Thank everyone that attended and link the articles so they can read and use as well especially if they were interviewed. Those attendees, whether they were sponsors, vendors or just out having fun, will love the fact that they were in the media as well. So you want to make sure they have the links to share on their own social media sites. When you have multiple people Tweeting, Facebooking, Intstagramming, it's going to raise awareness to who you are and what you're doing in the community.

For our annual Author Award Ceremony, we had *Good Life Tampa Bay* TV show come out for coverage of the event and interview the authors. This is another great way to get exposure for your event since they send a camera crew along with a reporter to interview authors, attendees and the hosts. Having someone interview your guests helps viewers gain another perspective of your book launch event. Obviously you want positive reviews so when you have that footage after the fact, people can see how awesome your event was so they will want to come out to other occasions in the future. You can watch our videos from all of our events on my website here:

http://richterpublishing.com/events/videos

INGREDIENT 7: SEO YOUR PARTY

You want to list your party on several event sites. But you don't just want it listed. You want a powerhouse event so momentous that when people search for a get-together online, your event is the first to pop up. Basically, you want to "Search Engine Optimize," or SEO, your party.

What is SEO? Search engines have Web spiders constantly updating the index of pages online. If you are searching for hand soap, Web spiders make sure the websites you find are related to hand soap. Search Engine Optimization is the process of maximizing the potential for people to see your event.

With the proper technique, you could rank your event on the first page of Google. When entering your event details, use key search terms that other people will use to find events in their area.

For my first party, I knew people were not going to Google "Tara Richter book launch party." Because I'm not famous and people will not be searching directly for me. This is one of the reasons I tied the event to Halloween. So when I posted my event on local forums or websites I could use several key search terms that people would be looking for:

- Tampa costume party
- Tampa Bay singles party
- Halloween book launch party
- Singles mixer Halloween costume party
- Halloween Tampa 2012

Have a strategy. Because I tied in the popular elements (Halloween, costumes, books, parties, prizes, singles, Tampa, etc.) my party came up first when you Googled Halloween Tampa 2012. My little ol' book signing party even came up higher in the search rankings than the Busch Gardens "Howl-O-Scream"—a major Halloween event in Tampa Bay! The fact that I got my party to rank higher than them on Google is mind blowing. But it shows you if you do it right, it can work!

The way that I accomplished this was by posting the party to as many free website listings as possible. There are many places online you can post your event. Make sure when you do list it, you properly place the appropriate keywords. Most listings always have a spot for "tags." Google online event websites in your local area. In Tampa Bay I use:

- 813area.com
- Craigslist.org
- Creative Loafing
- Event Live

Event Bright
Bay News 9 comm Calander
30 day in advance

Launch Your Book Into The Stratosphere & be a Best Seller!

INGREDIENT 8: SPONSORS

Let's face it, parties are expensive. No one wants to dig themselves deeper into debt while marketing their book. A great way to cover the cost of your event is by gaining sponsorship.

For my first party, I handed out tons of flyers. On the back of my flyer was a page full of advertised sponsors. For every ad, I earned money. In the end, the sponsorship covered the cost of all the flyers, and then some. Creative thinking like that can save money that would otherwise come out of your own pocket.

Barter for services. When you are trying to do a book launch on a shoe-string budget, bartering is your best friend. As I mentioned before, for my first party my hair stylist paid for an ad on the back of my flyer and gave away a big gift basket and gift certificate. For my second party he did my hair for free. In exchange, I let him set up business cards and flyers, and I created ads that rotated on the big TV screens in the venue.

He even gave away a gift basket.

At the second event, I also bartered with the draping company. They came to the bar and draped the walls, masking the neon beer signs. They installed lighting near the drapes. They covered the tables with linens. In exchange for their service, they gave out brochures and pamphlets about their business at the event, raffled off a gift basket and their ad displayed on the flat screens. Once again, you never know what you can get unless you ASK for it.

For my third event, everything was bartered. The cake was bartered in exchange for advertising. The PR for the event came from one of my authors. He did PR for the company, a win-win for him since he was selling his book at the event as well. We did not pay for the venue. We used one of our author's office space. Each author brought food and wine. The saxophonist was bartered because one of my authors gave the man free business services in exchange for the music.

The only thing we did not barter for was a photographer. Luckily, everyone with a smartphone took pictures, so we didn't need one. It was free publicity on social media. The pictures flooded Facebook. People emailed me about the next event based on those pictures alone. The only thing I paid out of pocket for was printing out fliers with Richter Publishing Packages for prospective authors to take home.

Remember: Bartering needs to be a win-win scenario to make it work.

INGREDIENT 9: FUN!

Make your event fun. The boring sit-at-a-table-and-autograph-the-book-people-were-waiting-in-line-to-buy-for-days are over. To get people out to your party, you need to have a fun event. This is especially true if you are a new author. Why should they come and see you?

For the *Dating Jungle* not only did we have costumes, prizes and drinks, we also had live jazz music. I decorated my area just like a jungle. Everything from a jungle background and vines hung all over the ceilings and tables, to blow-up monkeys to hang from the vines and palm trees on the walls. I even had a six foot Jane and Tarzan photo op printed where people could take pictures of themselves.

Think outside of the box. Don't be another boring book signing event. Do something crazy! The more over the top it is, the more people will have fun and remember it. Maybe bring a magician in to do card tricks or some kind of performer. For a children's book get a balloon artist. Anything to get people to stay and hang out for a while.

INGREDIENT 10: GREAT PHOTOS & VIDEOS

When you have such a great party, why not let people know about the fun time you had? Document everything that happens at your party. The more you have recorded, the more you can post online. The record increases your SEO and Google-ability when people post about your party.

Our last party received a ton of social media attention. People posted photos all over Facebook. So encourage your guests to take tons of photos and post them online—something most people already enjoy doing anyway!

It is also a good idea to hire a professional photographer. You do not want the only photos of your event to be badly-lit selfies. Social media posts are great, but if you're going to have a nice party, take some nice photos. It is worth the investment.

We have had some amazing videos taken at our parties. It's worth it to get them on tape and then edit it into a quick promo for you and your book/company. If you don't have a lot of extra money you can do it on your smartphone and then use a video editing software. However, if you can, hire a professional. Even if you're on a budget. You can never go back and document something that happened in the past. It's worth it to get that great video to post on your website, YouTube, Vimeo, etc. to get out into the world.

My video guy is AJ Favicchio with his company Sauce Digital (http://www.sauceontap.com/). He's fantastic! He videos the parties then makes cool short promos after. In this day and age we have very short attention spans. Some say humans have attention less than a gold fish—which is only about 5 second long. So we need to grab people's attention in this ever changing, quick downloading society. Because within a few moments someone may get distracted onto something else... squirrel! Check out his videos on my website here: http://richterpublishing.com/events/videos/

INGREDIENT 11: BECOME A BEST SELLER

Now that you have discovered all the ingredients to launch your book into the stratosphere and get the most amount of attention as possible, the next step is to make your book a Best Seller.

Everyone wants that status for their book. It's a feather to put in your cap for another accomplishment. There are millions of books published out there in the world. So how do you get *yours* to sell the most? Well, with anything there is a method to the madness. I'm going to share with you in this last chapter the steps I have taken to make some of my clients a Best Seller within Amazon.

Before I get into the nitty-gritty of this, let me first start off by saying nothing is certain. This strategy is a gamble. How do you win at poker? You must play the best hand. There's many different pieces of the puzzle in order to get your book of high rankings in the system. Yet, if one piece is misplaced at a certain time, you lose the game to a player with a better hand. I have proven the method works before, yet each time it is a gamble. However, in life if you want success and to be the best, there are risks involved.

There are two popular types of Best Seller statuses. Amazon Best Seller and New York Times Best Seller. Amazon Best Seller status comes from online sales within their market place. New York Times Best Seller comes from the book being bought within the physical book stores. Obviously, the second is much harder to gain. First you need your books to be carried by the bookstore, then you must get masses of people out to buy them. This is way easier if you are famous and have a lot of media attention around the release of your book. As we all know, getting people off their couch and physically into a bookstore in this digital age is much more difficult. Hence why Amazon is a much more viable answer for most authors. Customers can purchase directly from their smartphones. However, with that being said we are speaking of Best Seller status of paperback books being sold—not downloading Kindle versions. This status is for books bring printed and shipped out.

Here are the steps I have used successfully:

STEP #1 LIST YOUR BOOK IN A NICHE CATEGORY

Whether you are self-publishing or going through a publishing house, make sure your book is listed in an unusual category. You want to find the most niche sub-category you can for your book title. Why are we doing this? Because if you choose a very popular category, say Self-

Help/Motivational, that's a very popular category. If you go and look right now on Amazon Best Sellers in that category the authors that dominate top status are Tony Robbins, Napoleon Hill, and Stephen R. Covey. Do you want your book to compete with the big titles of *Think and Grow Rich* or *The 7 Habits of Highly Effective People*? No.

The truth is unless you're famous too, your book is not going to compete with these mega-sellers. Let's be honest with ourselves. Yes, flukes do happen like *Fifty Shades of Grey*, but it's much easier to get Best Seller status if you are NOT competing with another major book title.

So let's find a niche category that would be better for your title. Do a little research first. See who else is listed in that category before publishing. Who is your competition?

Look at the category: Self-Help/Handwriting Analysis. Not many big names in there. Actually none that I recognize at all. Who even knew that Handwriting Analysis was in Self-Help? That's definitely a niche category.

Now I know you may be saying, "Well, my self-help book doesn't fit into that category." I understand if it doesn't and that's an interesting filing for sure. However, the more unique it is, the better chance you have at selling more books than someone else.

Also, don't worry if your book won't pull up in searches with these "strange" listings because once it's a Best Seller it helps in search engines. Most of the time when you are promoting yourself on social media and such, you will be sending out the direct link for people to click and buy your book.

Getting reviews for your book helps it pull up as well. A strategy for that is to have all your friends and family write a review on Amazon for your book. All you need is an active account that you have purchased a product with. You do not have to purchase the item you are giving the review for. If you are in a writers group, have everyone in the group do a review for each other's books. There are companies you can pay to review your book. I haven't tested them out, so I'm not sure of their validity. But I know having reviews definitely helps and doesn't hurt your book (unless it's a really bad review).

STEP #2 CREATE AN AMAZON AUTHOR PAGE

Once your book is published, you want to go into Amazon and create an Author Page for yourself. Go here to set one up: https://authorcentral.amazon.com/

You want to set up your Amazon Author Page *before* you start your campaign because this will allow you to track your sales in real time.

Tip: You can create your Amazon Author Page before your book is published. However, you will not be able to claim the title as yours until it's available for sale on their site. It may take up to 24 hours before you can. If you cannot claim the title as yours, you cannot track sales.

The Author Page is also a great marketing tool because you can add all your books to it if you have written multiple. You can also upload any videos or TV interviews you've had. Write a bio about yourself and integrate your Twitter, Facebook or Blog feed so readers can get to know more about you. It even has an event spot where you can list book events! It's really a great tool to have once you are a published author. It will also enhance your Googleability because that page pulls up in search engines.

You can see my author page as an example here: http://www.amazon.com/Tara-Richter/e/B00CGKD8FG

STEP #3 SELL AS MANY BOOKS IN THE SHORTEST TIME FRAME

Now this is the difficult part. You need to outsell all other authors in your category at any given time frame. Hence why you don't want that many other books listed in your category. Because you have no idea how many people are buying their books. The less popular they are, probably the least amount are being sold. Just a theory.

Tip: The books that go into Best Seller status are the ones from the consumer side. When you self-publish you can buy your own books at wholesale cost within their system as the author or publisher. However, these sales DO NOT go into account for books being sold for Best Seller status. This is just for your own personal use. It's the amount of books by the customers in Amazon's market place.

So there are a few ways to accomplish this.

A) **Do a hard hitting email campaign:** When you get ready to release your book, set a date and tell everyone you know to purchase on that day of release. Get people excited about it! Tell everyone a week ahead of time, so they know what day to purchase your book.

B) **Social media campaign:** Create an ad on Facebook with the direct link to purchase the book and run it the day of your release with a targeted crowd that would be interested in buying your type of book. If you're pushing a book on retirement, you wouldn't want to market it to people in their 20's. They don't care about retirement. Your target audience would be people in their 50's or 60's that are right on the verge of starting the second half of their life. Blast your release date on other social media sites as well such as Twitter, LinkedIn, Google+, etc.

C) **Make an event page:** Create an event within Facebook and invite people to it. Make it public so people can share with their friends as well. The cool thing about FB events is that every time you upload a photo or make an announcement within the event page, everyone who you invited to it will get a notification. I use this technique with my workshops and other book events as well. I create the event about a week ahead of time and add everyone. Then three days prior I post a short 60 second promo video, the day before a reminder, then the day of it will remind everyone in the system. Facebook somehow will even end up on people's smartphone calendars. I don't even know how that works. But in my iPhone sometimes I will see everyone else's FB events pull up. I'm sure it's somewhere in the settings. It can be annoying, but good for marketing purposes.

Tip: Once your book is *published* it takes anywhere from 3-7 days to show up in the Amazon market to be purchased. DO NOT launch your campaign before you see it listed in there yourself! Otherwise all your efforts will go down the drain because no one will actually be able to buy it yet.

STEP #4 MONITOR YOUR RESULTS

After you have put all the items in place and launched your campaigns, then comes the waiting game. This is the not-so-fun part. Sitting back and hoping all your efforts pay off. The thing that really kind of stinks is Amazon doesn't even notify you when you do hit Best Seller status. I suppose it's because they have so many. Needless to say it would be nice to receive a notification at some point in time. Yet, you're left to anxiously watch and refresh the Best Seller list of your chosen category waiting like a school girl hoping that cute boy will call. Starring at the phone to ring—like if you stare hard and long enough your psychic powers will make it magically chime.

Tip: Category rankings appear in the Product Details section of a book's detail page only if the book is ranked in the Top 100 books in its category.

What this means is that if your book hits the top 100 in its category, it is considered a Best Seller, but you can only see this on the product details page of your book. So that's why we must keep refreshing your product details page and Amazon's Best Seller list.

Amazon does update their list online every hour. Unfortunately, that doesn't mean it will take an hour to see if you've hit the list. From my experience it can take anywhere up to 10-12 hours to see the results of your campaign. So it's imperative that you keep watching! We are looking for Best Seller of your niche category. Or a Hot New Release.

Amazon only puts a status next to your book if you've reached **#1 Best Seller**. In order to receive that status normally you are also a New York Times Bester Seller and you've sold about 3,000-5,000 books a day (roughly) on a consistent basis.

We are just trying to get your book in the top 100 list. Yet, this is still a Best Seller Status. So the good thing is once you hit it, you can still advertise it as such.

I used this method with one of my authors I published, *The Book on Retirement* by Kevin Houser and Gary Plessl. We coordinated the marketing launch and the book made #3 in Amazon Hot New Releases and #62 in Amazon Best Sellers in the category of *Business & Money/Personal Finance/Retirement Planning*.

So now we can leverage that when doing media and TV interviews for their book. You only need to hit Best Seller once and you're golden!

Launch Your Book Into The Stratosphere & be a Best Seller!

OUR AUTHORS

Some of our authors include:

Anthony Amos with Shark Bites by Kevin Harrington
Pierce Brunson
Genevieve Dobson
Meredith Rodgers
Elizabeth Bunbury
James Chittenden
Joseph Warren

To purchase books by our authors visit:
http://richterpublishing.com/featured-authors/

WRITE A BOOK IN 4 WEEKS!

ABOUT THE AUTHOR

Tara Richter is the President of Richter Publishing LLC and specializes in helping business owners write their non-fiction story in 4 weeks and publish a book in order to establish themselves as an expert in their industry. She has been featured on *CNN, ABC, Daytime TV, FOX, SSN, Channel 10 News, USA TODAY* and *Beverly Hills Times.*

Her degree is in Graphic Design and she worked in the copy and print industry in the Silicon Valley. She has written and published 11 of her own books in just a few short years. Tara now has published many authors including Anthony Amos and celebrity entrepreneur, Kevin Harrington, Shark from ABC's "Shark Tank," with their joint book, "How to Catch a Shark."

Tara was a finalist for Tampa Bay's Business Woman of the Year Awards, nominee for Tampa's Up & Coming Businesses & nominee for Iconic Woman Entrepreneur of the Year.

Richter Publishing LLC has streamlined the complex writing and publishing industry so anyone can become a published author in just a few weeks!

For more information on becoming an author contact us at www.richterpublishing.com

To purchase Tara's other books visit:
http://www.amazon.com/Tara-Richter/e/B00CGKD8FG/

Made in the USA
Lexington, KY
09 April 2015